Northern Ireland

Good Food is in our Nature

A collection of recipes

Introduction

The Royal Ulster Agricultural Society welcomes the opportunity to join with four of the sectors in the Northern Ireland food supply chain to help spread the message that "good food is in our nature."

Agri-food production plays a central role in the Northern Ireland private sector economy, representing 20% of our turnover.

This book of "good food" recipes is our first joint initiative. It sets out to encourage aspiring teenage cooks, time pressed mothers and even traditional northern man to get into the kitchen. We've tried to make it easy. In most cases no great culinary skill is required so everyone giving it a try will turn out dishes which are quicker and easier than many convenience foods. There are also a few recipes for the more adventurous chefs who simply fancy a change.

We all want healthier and more nutritious meals and this book shows you how to get started. The fresh local ingredients used in the recipes all form part of a healthy diet. We need to think about the balance of the meals we prepare at home so the nutritional benefits of the ingredients are outlined at the beginning of each section.

And finally, it needn't cost more, and it doesn't cost more to eat healthily – as you'll find when you try these dishes.

Livestock Commission – Beef & Lamb

We live in a constantly changing world where nothing stands still for long. Despite today's hectic lifestyles, what we eat has never been more important to us, and we demand that our food is as natural and wholesome as it can be, providing all the nutrients we need to keep us fit for life.

No single food contains all the nutrients needed for health, so it is recommended that we eat a balanced diet containing a wide variety of different foods. Lean red meats are an important source of iron and zinc, high quality protein, B vitamins, and a range of other nutrients essential for optimal health at every stage of life. Today's beef & lamb are also much lower in fat that ever before, and lean cuts can form an important part of a balanced diet.

Look for the Northern Ireland Farm Quality Assured logo when you purchase beef and lamb and you can be sure that your meat is safe, healthy, wholesome and natural.

The Northern Ireland Farm Quality Assurance Scheme is a code of practice for beef & lamb farmers. This quality code operates to a European Standard (EN45011) and is recognised by everyone as giving real assurance about the quality of the farm and methods used in the production of your beef and lamb. Northern Ireland Farm Quality Assured animals are fed on our famous Northern Ireland grass, providing meat which is higher in Omega 3 fatty acids than cereal fed animals.

The scheme covers all aspects of production including stockmanship and animal welfare, animal health, nutrition, housing and handling, right through to care for the environment. Look out for the logo when buying beef and lamb and you can be sure of the highest European standards.

Beef Bourguignonne

Serves 4
Cooking time: 2 ½ hours
Temperature: 190°C, 375°F, Gas mark 5

Ingredients:

- 450g (1 lb) Northern Ireland Farm Quality Assured steak, cut into 2.5cm (1 inch) pieces
- 15ml (1 tbsp) olive oil
- 1 medium onion (peeled and chopped finely)
- 1 large carrot (peeled and chopped finely)
- 1-2 garlic cloves (crushed)
- 15ml (1 tbsp) plain white flour
- 15ml (1 tbsp) tomato purée
- 300ml (½ pt) red wine
- 300ml (½ pt) brown stock
- bouquet garni, (parsley stalk, bay leaf, thyme)
- seasoning
- 15ml (1 tbsp) olive oil
- 250g (8 oz) shallots (peeled)
- 125g (4 oz) button mushrooms (wiped)
- 150ml (¼ pt) red wine
- parsley to garnish

Method:

1 Heat the oil in a large non-stick wok or saucepan and fry the beef until lightly browned, remove with a slotted spoon and place in a casserole dish.
2 Add the carrots, onions and garlic to the wok or saucepan and fry until the onions are a golden colour, add the flour and stir well, add to the meat.
3 Pour the stock and 300ml red wine into the wok or saucepan, bring to the boil. Pour over the meat.
4 Add the tomato purée, bouquet garni, salt and pepper to the casserole, stir well, cover and cook in a preheated oven for 1½ to 2 hours.
5 Heat half of the remaining oil in a saucepan and fry the mushrooms until lightly browned and remove from the saucepan.
6 Heat the rest of the oil and fry the shallots until browned, add the wine and cook until the shallots are just tender.
7 When the meat is cooked, remove the bouquet garni, add the mushrooms and shallots, check seasoning and cook for a further 20 to 25 minutes.
8 Sprinkle with chopped parsley and serve with vegetables and potatoes.

Serves 4
Cooking time: 20 minutes

Italian Steak Wrap

Ingredients:

- 450g (1 lb) Northern Ireland Farm Quality Assured lean beef (thinly sliced)
- 2 cloves garlic (crushed)
- 6 sundried tomatoes (drained and chopped)
- 5ml (1 tsp) oil from sundried tomatoes
- 100g (4 oz) chestnut mushrooms (wiped and sliced)
- seasoning
- 6-8 cherry tomatoes (quartered)
- 2 x 15ml (2 tbsp) half fat crème fraîche
- 1 pack of flour tortillas

Method:

1 Heat oil in a non-stick pan. Add the meat and garlic. Cook thoroughly. Remove from the pan and keep warm.
2 Add the sundried tomatoes and mushrooms to the pan and cook until mushrooms are slightly softened. Add the cherry tomatoes, crème fraîche and seasoning. Heat very gently for 1 minute (tomatoes should keep their shape).
3 Heat the wraps in the microwave oven (approximately 40 seconds at medium power).
4 Place spoonfuls of the meat filling into the middle of each wrap.
5 Fold up the base and then fold in each side to form a pocket.
6 Serve garnished with a side salad.

Lamb Chops with Honey

Serves 4

Cooking time: approximately 16-19 minutes

Ingredients:

- 4 Northern Ireland Farm Quality
  Assured loin lamb chops
- 15g butter
- 4 x 5ml (4 tsp) chopped fresh
  mint –
  or 2 x 5ml (2 tsp) of dried mint
- 3 x 15ml (3 tbsp) clear honey
- 3ml (½ tsp) grated lemon rind

Method:

1 Dot the chops with half the butter and grill for 8 to 10 minutes
   or until browned.
2 Turn and cook the other side for 3 or 4 minutes.
3 Combine the mint, honey and lemon rind and spread on the
   meat.
4 Cook for another 5 minutes.

Rack of Lamb

with rosemary & mustard crust

Serves 3
Cooking time: 45-50 minutes
Temperature: 190°C, 375°F, Gas mark 5

Ingredients:

- 450g (1 lb) Northern Ireland
  Farm Quality Assured lamb rack
- 15ml (1 tbsp) oil
- 15g butter
- 4 shallots (finely chopped)
- 50g breadcrumbs
- 5ml (1 tsp) dried rosemary
- 15ml (1 tbsp) Dijon mustard

Method:

1 Preheat oven to 190°C/375°F/Gas mark 5.
2 Place the lamb rack in a frying pan and seal on all sides.
  Transfer the rack to a roasting tin.
3 Heat the oil and butter in the same frying pan. Sauté the shallots
  for 2 minutes.
4 Add the breadcrumbs and rosemary and cook for a further 2
  minutes.
5 Brush the lamb rack with the Dijon mustard, and pack the crumb
  crust on top.
6 Place in the oven and cook for 45-50 minutes. Allow to stand for
  10 minutes.
7 Cut into cutlets and serve.

Stir Fried Beef

Serves 2
Cooking time: 10 minutes

Ingredients:

- 225g (8 oz) Northern Ireland Farm Quality Assured rump steak (sliced thinly)
- 5ml (1 tsp) soy sauce
- 5ml (1 tsp) five spice powder
- 5ml (1 tsp) oil

- 2 cloves of garlic (crushed)
- 2.5cm (1 inch) ginger (peeled and grated)
- 5ml (1 tsp) oil

- 1 carrot (peeled and sliced into thin strips)

- ½ red pepper (sliced thinly)
- 60g (2 oz) broccoli florets
- 60g (2 oz) mange tout (sliced thinly)
- ½ medium onion (sliced thinly)

(Alternative to preceding 5 ingredients:
1 packet Chinese stir fry vegetables)

- 5ml (1 tsp) cornflour
- 150ml (¼ pt) water
- 15ml (1 tbsp) soy sauce
- 5ml (1 tsp) chilli sauce

Method:

1. Place the steak, soy sauce and five spice powder into a bowl and mix well.
2. Heat one teaspoonful of oil in a non-stick wok until very hot, stir fry the meat for 2 or 3 minutes until browned, transfer to a plate and keep warm.
3. Wipe the wok, heat one teaspoonful of oil and fry the garlic and ginger for 1 minute.
4. Add the vegetables and stir fry for 3 to 4 minutes, add the meat.
5. Mix the cornflour with water, soy sauce, chilli sauce and stir well.
6. Add to the meat and vegetable mixture over high heat, stir well until the sauce thickens, serve hot with egg noodles or steamed rice and prawn crackers.

Topped Steaks

Serves 2

Steak:

In a non-stick frying pan dry fry 2 Northern Ireland Farm Quality Assured lean grilling/frying steaks according to taste. When cooked remove from pan and keep warm.

Sauce:

Onion & garlic creamy sauce
- Add to the pan ½ red onion (sliced) and fry, add 50g (2 oz) soft garlic and herb cream cheese, 6 x 15ml (6 tbsp) semi-skimmed milk. Heat gently for approximately 1 minute.
- Stir through 15ml (1 tbsp) chives, chopped.

Pesto sauce
- Add to the pan 2 x 15ml (2 tbsp) half fat crème fraîche, 2 x 15ml (2 tbsp) semi-skimmed milk, 15ml (1 tbsp) red or green pesto. Heat gently for 1 minute.
- Stir through 4 olives, pitted and chopped and 15ml (1 tbsp) fresh basil, roughly chopped.

Creamy chilli sauce
- Add to the pan 50g (2oz) soft cream cheese, 6 x 15ml (6 tbsp) semi-skimmed milk.
- Heat gently for approximately 1 minute. Stir through 10 cherry tomatoes, halved and 5ml (1 tsp) chilli powder or sweet chilli sauce (more if you like it hot).

Stilton and watercress sauce
- Add to the pan 3 x 15ml (3 tbsp) half fat crème fraîche, 50g (2 oz) stilton cheese, crumbled. Heat gently for 1 minute. Stir through 25g (1 oz) watercress, roughly chopped, until wilted.

Cranberry and camembert topping
- Spread 2 x 15ml (2 tbsp) cranberry sauce over the top of the steak, then top with camembert cheese.
- Serve with mixed green salad, asparagus and new potatoes.

Serve steaks with sauce of your choice, crispy oven baked chips and onions, new potatoes, or pre-prepared mashed potato and vegetables.

Northern
Ireland
Seafood

Northern Ireland Seafood

Northern Ireland enjoys an enviable reputation for some of the highest quality fresh produce in the world and, in particular, we have a wide choice of seafood and speciality products that provide you, the consumer, with a versatile range of healthy and nutritious dishes. The lakes and surrounding seas abound with a wealth of natural goodness and our location on the west of Europe puts Northern Ireland in a prime location to supply quality fish and shellfish.

Fish is an excellent source of protein, which is essential for growth and repair, and the maintenance of muscles and body tissues. It contains Vitamin A, which helps to maintain healthy eyes, skin, and hair and Vitamin D that is required to help the formation of strong bones.

White fish such as Whiting and Monkfish are very low in calories while oily fish such as Salmon, Mackerel and Herring contain Omega 3 fatty acids, which are essential for good health. Research in trials of school children has suggested that a greater intake of Omega 3 in many cases improved co-ordination, concentration and academic ability. It can also help the brain to develop and prevent a number of conditions including heart disease, dyslexia, asthma, dyspraxia and ADHD.

Our abundant natural resources are backed by considerable experience in food processing, first-class production environments, hygiene controls and a commitment to service and sustainable supplies.

There is no better time to enjoy the taste of fish!

Caramelised
Pan Seared Trout

with lemongrass & chilli honey glaze

Serves 2

Ingredients:

- fresh fillets of Sea Trout/Trout or Salmon
- 2 x 15ml (2 tbsp) sesame oil
- 2 x 15ml (2 tbsp) heather honey
- 3 x 15ml (3 tbsp) dark soy sauce
- 25g (1 oz) shredded red chilli pepper
- 25g (1 oz) shredded lemongrass
- 25g (1 oz) fresh peeled ginger (sliced into thin strips)
- 25g (1 oz) garlic cloves (peeled and sliced)
- fresh limes
- 25g (1 oz) fresh coriander sprigs

Method:

1 Combine the sesame, honey and soy together. Crush up all the chilli, lemongrass, ginger and garlic and rub generously over your fish fillets. Marinate in the liquid for approximately 1 hour, covered to retain all the mouth-watering aromas.
2 Preheat your pan, grill or barbecue and cook fillets until a rich caramelised golden brown, with a delicious sticky glaze and still pinkish in the centre.
3 Drizzle with lime juice, sprinkle with coriander sprigs and serve.

Serves 2
Cooking time: 19 minutes

Kids' Kedgeree

Ingredients:

- 1 medium onion (diced)
- 5ml (1 tsp) vegetable oil
- 200g (8 oz) long grain rice (rinsed)
- 15ml (1 tbsp) "korma" curry powder
- 275ml (½ pt) milk
- 275ml (½ pt) water
- ½ chicken stock cube
- 200g (8 oz) smoked white fish (diced small)
- 50g (2 oz) frozen peas
- 1 fresh mango diced (optional)
- 60g (2 oz) butter

Method:

1 Fry onions over medium heat until soft.
2 Add rice and curry powder.
3 Stir in the milk, water and stock cube.
4 Cover with a tight fitting lid and simmer for 10 minutes.
5 Add fish and cook for a further 2 minutes.
6 Add peas, mango and butter then stir for 2 minutes.
7 Serve in a warm bowl.

Kircubbin Bay Crab Claws

with lemon, garlic and chilli
Serves 2

Ingredients:

- 75g (3 oz) butter
- 1 red chilli deseeded and finely chopped
- 2 cloves of garlic (finely chopped)
- ½ lemon in wedges
- 10-12 Crab claws (depending on appetites)
- coriander or similar herb (finely chopped)
- salt and pepper

Method:

1 Firstly crack Crab claws and discard excess shell.
2 Now melt the butter and add garlic and chilli, gently sweat. Add the Crab, toss and turn to a high heat, for 30 seconds.
3 Next add coriander to taste, season with salt, pepper and a squeeze of lemon.
4 Ready to serve with a wedge of lemon.

Salmon Quesadilla

with cream cheese & chives
Serves 2

Ingredients:

- 2 boneless, skinless Salmon fillets
- salt and pepper
- vegetable oil for cooking

- 4 x 20cm (8 inch) flour plain tortillas
- 1 tub of cream cheese
- 1 packet of fresh chives (thinly sliced)

Method:

1 Lightly season the Salmon fillets with salt and pepper. Brush with oil and cook under a hot grill. Cool, flake and set aside.
2 Spread each tortilla lightly with cream cheese and sprinkle with chives.
3 On one half of the tortilla divide the Salmon equally.
4 Fold over the tortilla and in a large frying pan over a medium heat fry the quesadilla until golden brown on both sides.
5 To serve cut into triangles and serve with potato salad and salsa.

Strangford Lobster

with fresh linguini, summer vegetables, roast shellfish oil & chilli gremolata

Serves 2

Ingredients:

- 2 x cooked Lobsters (meat removed, and diced: retain Lobster shells)
- 15ml (1 tbsp) tomato purée
- 2 x 15ml (2 tbsp) extra virgin olive oil

- 2 portions of fresh pasta
- 1 medium courgette
- 4 asparagus spears
- 100g (4 oz) spinach
- 2 artichokes

For the Chilli Gremolata
- 2 x 15ml (2 tbsp) chopped parsley
- 15ml (1 tbsp) chopped red chillies

- 15ml (1 tbsp) chopped lemon zest
- 15ml (1 tbsp) minced garlic

Method:

1. Roast Lobster shells with tomato purée in a little olive oil for 30 minutes.
2. Deglaze with a glass of white wine and add 2 tbsp of extra virgin olive oil.
3. Season and strain the liquid.
4. Make chilli gremolata by stirring chopped parsley, red chillies, lemon zest and minced garlic in a small bowl.
5. Cook vegetables.
6. Warm pasta and summer vegetables and place in a bowl with cooked Lobster and retained liquid.
7. Sprinkle chilli gremolata over the top.

Spicy Prawn Salad

Serves 2

Ingredients:

- 200g (8 oz) Prawns
- ½ avocado (peeled and diced 2cm)
- 50g (2 oz) cherry tomatoes (cut in half)

- 50g (2 oz) cooked green beans
- 2 soft boiled eggs (quartered)
- 2 x 15ml (2 tbsp) chives (chopped)
- salt and cracked black pepper
- 1 bottle French dressing
- salad leaves to serve

For the Sauce
- 100ml (¼ pt) mayonnaise
- 2 x 15ml (2 tbsp) tomato ketchup
- 15ml (1 tbsp) lemon juice

- 5ml (1 tsp) paprika
- 2 x 5ml (2 tsp) English mustard
- 3ml (½ tsp) chilli powder

Method:

1 Mix all ingredients for sauce together.
2 In a bowl, place Prawns, avocado, tomatoes, green beans, eggs and chives. Season with salt and cracked black pepper and drizzle with a little French dressing.
3 Drizzle sauce onto a large plate. Arrange Prawns and vegetables around the outside. Arrange the salad leaves in the centre of the plate and drizzle some more sauce over the Prawns and vegetables. Serve.

Ulster Pork and Bacon Forum

The Ulster Pork & Bacon Forum is an industry trade and marketing organisation for the pigmeat sector of Northern Ireland. Our events and activities are funded jointly by local pig producers and processors.

The Forum's marketing strategies promote local pork all year-round and achieve extensive coverage by differentiating local produce. We liaise closely with the supply-chain to bring you the very best of pork and bacon and select product ranges available in Northern Ireland.

HEALTH FACT
Pork is leaner than ever! The average fat content of 100g of fully trimmed lean, raw pork is just 3.7g. Some cuts of pork, such as leg, can contain as little as 1.7g fat per 100g. Surprisingly perhaps, this means that pork can contain less fat than salmon. More than 50% of the fat present in pork is unsaturated. Unsaturated fats are considered healthier and are associated with a lower risk of heart disease.

Recipes to savour...
Pork tastes fantastic simply on its own or try it combined with garlic, honey, soya, apple, ginger, chilli, pineapple, rosemary and spices from all over the globe. We have really enjoyed developing these six new recipes for you using top quality pork and bacon products from Northern Ireland. We hope you are tempted to try some of the recipes in your own kitchen!

'Thank Goodness' is an industry endorsement for local pork produce. When buying local pork, bacon, ham and sausage products you are directly supporting producers and processors from farm to plate, and are guaranteed high standards of animal welfare, quality assurance and traceability.

Roasted Thai Style

Red Pork

with sticky coconut rice and a chilli dipping sauce

Serves 2
Cooking time: 45 minutes–1 hour
Temperature: 180°C, 250°F, Gas mark 4

Ingredients:

- 450g (1 lb) whole pork fillet

For the Marinade
- 2 cloves of garlic (crushed)
- 3cms (1 inch) root ginger (grated)
- 15ml (1 tbsp) dark soy sauce
- 15ml (1 tbsp) hoi-sin sauce
- 15ml (1 tbsp) sesame oil
- 15ml (1 tbsp) soft brown sugar
- 5ml (1 tsp) five spice powder

For the Coconut Rice
- 225g (8 oz) long grain rice
- 400ml (¾ pt) coconut milk

For the Dipping Sauce
- 3 x 15ml (3 tbsp) dark soy sauce
- 1 red chilli (de-seeded and finely chopped)

To Serve
- 1 fresh lime
- a few spring onions

Method:

1 Mix all the marinade ingredients together and pour over the pork fillet. Cover and leave to marinate for an hour or overnight in the fridge, if possible.
2 Remove the pork from the marinade, reserving the remainder for basting. Place the pork in a roasting tin, cover the tin with foil and cook in a moderate oven for 45 minutes to 1 hour, basting occasionally.
3 Cook the rice in 500ml (1 pt) boiling water until the water has almost evaporated.
4 Add the coconut milk to the rice and season to taste. Continue to cook until the rice is 'sticky'.
5 Mix in a little chopped chilli and coriander for colour.
6 To serve, cut or tear the pork into strips, pour over the juices and serve with dipping sauce, slices of fresh lime and spring onions.

Quick and Easy

Italian Frittata

with crispy bacon and spinach

Serves 4
Pre-heat the grill to a moderate heat

Ingredients:

- 125g (4 oz) smoked bacon
  (cut into small cubes)
- 7ml (½ tbsp) butter
- 7 large eggs* (lightly beaten
  and well-seasoned)
- 1 potato (peeled, cooked
  and cut into cubes)
- 2 handfuls of spinach

Method:

1 Dry fry the bacon in a non-stick frying pan over a moderate heat
   until crispy.
2 Remove from the pan and set aside. Add the butter to the pan.
   When ready, add the beaten eggs, bacon, potato and spinach
   and stir gently until the bottom starts to set.
3 Cook for 5-10 minutes and then finish off under the grill until
   set.
4 To serve, invert onto a serving plate so that you see a nice
   golden top. Cut into wedges.

*Eggs: The taste will vary depending on the quality of the eggs you
buy. Aim for free-range, but organic is even better.

Honey Grilled
Pork Sausages
with colcannon mash and onion gravy

Serves 4

Ingredients:

- 16 pork sausages
- vegetable oil
- honey

For the Onion Gravy
- 30g (1 oz) onions (sliced)
- 3ml (½ tsp) rubbed sage
- 10g (½ oz) butter
- 3 x 15ml (3 tbsp) red wine
- 250ml (½ pt) pork or vegetable stock

For the Colcannon Mash
- 50g (2 oz) savoy cabbage
- 50g (2 oz) streaky bacon
- 10g (½ oz) butter
- 350g (12 oz) mashed potatoes
- 25g (1 oz) chopped scallions

Method:

1 Put the sausages in a bowl and toss with a little honey and vegetable oil.
2 Grill the sausages until golden brown and cooked through. Put to one side and keep warm.
3 While the sausages are grilling, make the gravy by frying the onions, sage and butter in a pan until golden brown.
4 Deglaze the pan with the red wine and add the stock.
5 Reduce gravy until thickened (you can add a little more butter if you wish to correct the consistency). Keep warm until serving.
6 For the colcannon, fry the butter, cabbage and bacon in a pan until cooked through.
7 Add the cooked mashed potatoes and beat until warmed through, then add the scallions.
8 Place the colcannon in the centre of a large plate and top with the pork sausages. Serve piping hot with the onion gravy.

Pork and
Pineapple Curry

with rice, mango chutney and naan bread

Serves 4

Ingredients:

- 1kg (2 lb) lean pork (cubed)
- 40g (2 oz) flour
- 5ml (1 tsp) salt
- 2 x 15ml (2 tbsp) cooking oil
- 1 large onion (chopped)
- 15ml (1 tbsp) Madras curry paste
- 15ml (1 tbsp) paprika
- 300ml (½ pt) chicken stock
- 2 dried red chillies
- 15ml (1 tbsp) mango chutney
- 5ml (1 tsp) Worcester sauce
- 400g (14 oz) tin pineapple cubes (in their syrup)
- 2 bay leaves
- Boiled rice, 4 naan bread and mango chutney

Method:

1 Toss the pork in the flour and salt.
2 In a large pan heat the oil and brown the meat.
3 When the meat has turned a nice golden colour, lift out onto a plate with a draining spoon and leave to one side.
4 In the same pan, leave some fat from cooking the pork and gently fry the onion until soft. Stir in the curry paste and paprika.
5 Fry for two minutes then return the browned meat to the pan. Stir well and cook for a few more minutes.
6 To finish the dish, add all the remaining ingredients and bring to the boil. Once boiled, reduce the heat to a simmer, cover with a lid and continue cooking on the hob for 1 hour or until the pork is tender.
7 When ready, remove the bay leaves and serve with plain boiled rice and naan bread with a side dish of mango chutney.

Sautéed Tender

Pork Fillet

with caramelised apricots and a sweet garlic drizzle

Serves 4

Temperature: 180°C, 250°F, Gas mark 4

Ingredients:

- 600g (1½ lb) pork fillet
- salt and black pepper
- vegetable oil
- 50g (2 oz) onion (finely chopped)
- 1 clove garlic (crushed)
- 3 x 15ml (3 tbsp) red wine
- 125ml (¼ pt) pork or vegetable stock

- 10g (½ oz) butter (ice cold)
- chopped parsley

For the Caramelised Apricots
- 200g (8 oz) dried apricots
- 10ml (1 dsp) maple syrup

Method:

1 Cut the pork fillet into round medallions or tiny steaks and season with salt and pepper.
2 In a non-stick pan, sauté the pork fillet in vegetable oil until lightly browned. Place in a roasting tin in the oven for 15 minutes until the juices run clear then remove and keep warm.
3 In another pan over a medium heat, gently fry the chopped onion and garlic until golden brown.
4 Add the red wine and stock and slowly boil down until the liquid is reduced by half.
5 Remove the garlic jus from the heat and add small knobs of ice cold butter. Whisk in the butter to end up with a rich glossy sauce. Add the finely chopped parsley.
6 Melt the maple syrup in a saucepan and add the apricots. Lower the heat and cook for a few minutes until the apricots are caramelised.
7 Serve the pork with caramelised apricots and drizzle with the sweet garlic jus.

Tip: This is great served with a fresh green salad and new potatoes.

Sticky Sesame

Pork Kebabs

with chargrilled vegetables and zesty rice

Serves 4

Ingredients:

- 450g (1 lb) pork fillet (cubed)
- 1 garlic clove (crushed)
- 2.5cm (1 inch) ginger (peeled and grated)
- 1 red chilli (finely chopped)
- 15ml (1 tbsp) clear honey

- 2 x 15ml (2 tbsp) dark soy sauce
- 2 x 15ml (2 tbsp) sherry
- 2 x 15ml (2 tbsp) sesame oil
- cherry tomatoes, courgettes, onions and red peppers (cubed)

For the zesty rice
- 300g (10 oz) long grain rice
- a pinch of salt
- 2 x 15ml (2 tbsp) fresh coriander

- 1 lime (grated zest of)
- 15ml (1 tbsp) sesame seeds (toasted)

Method:

1. Soak 8 wooden skewers for 30 minutes in a bowl of water to prevent them from burning under the grill.
2. Put the pork in a dish with the garlic, ginger, chilli, honey, soy sauce, sherry and sesame oil and mix together well.
3. Cover and leave to marinate for 15 minutes.
4. Thread the pork and the chopped vegetables alternately onto the skewers and grill for 12-15 minutes under a medium heat, turning frequently.
5. Put the rice in a large saucepan with 400ml of water and a pinch of salt. Bring to the boil, then reduce the heat.
6. Cover and simmer without stirring for 12 minutes and remove from the heat.
7. Fluff up the grains with a fork and mix in the coriander and lime zest.
8. To serve, divide the rice between four warmed plates. Top each with two kebabs and scatter with the toasted sesame seeds.

Pure Northern Ireland Dairy Products

Northern Ireland has few natural resources - but it has some: an abundant supply of water, and an ability to grow grass. The main food of dairy cows in Northern Ireland is grass, whether at pasture during April to October, or as silage when cows are housed during the winter months. It is from this natural resource of grass that milk is produced on dairy farms throughout Northern Ireland.

Dairy farming is a job that requires commitment - it's an all day, every day job. Dairy cows have to be milked twice a day, every day. As well as commitment, skill and knowledge are required to be a successful dairy farmer - knowing when grass is ready to cut for silage, planning investment to improve efficiency and animal welfare, and working with nature in each season. Most young dairy farmers spend time at college, but much of the skills and knowledge are handed down from generation to generation.

As well as working with nature, dairy farming is about the relationship between the farmer and his animals. That is why dairy farmers in Northern Ireland operate the Five Freedoms of Animal Welfare:
- freedom from hunger and thirst,
- freedom from discomfort,
- freedom from pain injury or disease,
- freedom to express normal behaviour,
- freedom from fear and distress

All of these - commitment, skills, knowledge, and high standards of animal welfare - contribute to the very high quality of milk produced on dairy farms. The quality of Northern Ireland milk is amongst the highest in the world – it is six times better than required by the EU.

And because of this high quality, Northern Ireland dairy products are in demand around the world. In fact, the Northern Ireland dairy industry exports to over 100 countries around the world.

So enjoy the recipes in the following pages, in the knowledge that Northern Ireland dairy products are amongst the best in the world.

Recipes from this section are from the "Year Round Dairy Cookbook"
Dairy Cookbooks can be ordered from www.dairydiary.co.uk or on 01536 762922

Nutrition

Essential nutrients

Milk and dairy products are an important part of a healthy, balanced diet. As well as being packed with bone-building calcium, *milk, cheese* and *yogurt* provide a host of other essential nutrients including protein, vitamin A, B-vitamins, phosphorus, magnesium and zinc. These have benefits ranging from helping to keep skin healthy to maintaining normal muscle function and eye health.

Bone health

Milk and dairy products are some of the best natural sources of calcium, essential for bone health. Three servings of dairy foods - for example, a glass of milk, a pot of yogurt and a small (matchbox-sized) piece of cheese - will provide all the calcium most people need each day. Dairy foods also supply other nutrients that are important for bone health including zinc, magnesium, phosphorus and protein.

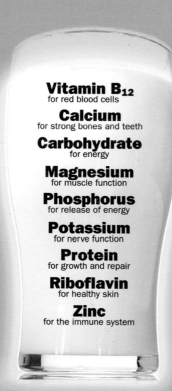

Vitamin B₁₂
for red blood cells

Calcium
for strong bones and teeth

Carbohydrate
for energy

Magnesium
for muscle function

Phosphorus
for release of energy

Potassium
for nerve function

Protein
for growth and repair

Riboflavin
for healthy skin

Zinc
for the immune system

Dental health

Eating a small piece of cheese after a meal can help neutralise harmful acid in the mouth and so help prevent tooth decay. Milk is tooth-friendly too; apart from water, it's the only drink recommended by dentists as safe between meals.

Blood pressure

High blood pressure is a risk factor for heart disease and stroke. The DASH eating plan, which includes three servings of low-fat dairy foods a day and five portions of fruit and vegetables has been shown to help lower blood pressure.

Weight control

Evidence is emerging that dairy foods may help with weight control and could make it easier to lose weight. A series of studies has found that including three to four servings of low-fat dairy foods a day as part of a calorie-controlled diet helps people to lose more weight than cutting calories alone on a low-dairy diet.

Savoury Pancake Stack

Serves 4
Cooking time: 30 minutes
Temperature: 200°C, 400°F, Gas mark 6

Ingredients:

For the Pancakes (makes 8):
- 125g (4½ oz) plain flour
- 1 large egg
- 300ml (½ pint) milk
- 2 x 15ml (2 tbsp) sunflower oil for cooking

For the filling:
- 200g (7 oz) thick bacon, (de-rinded and diced)
- 1 onion (peeled and diced)
- oil to cook

- 150g (5oz) cup mushrooms (wiped and chopped)
- salt and freshly ground black pepper
- 5 x 15ml (5 tbsp) chopped parsley

For the sauce:
- 40g (1½ oz) butter
- 40g (1½ oz) plain flour
- 450ml (¾ pint) milk
- 15ml (1 tbsp) coarse grain mustard
- 50g (2oz) mature cheddar cheese (grated)

Method:

1 To make pancakes, put flour into a large bowl, add egg and half the milk. Mix with a hand mixer until bubbly. Stir in rest of milk.

2 Add a few drops of oil to an 18–20cm (7–8 inch) shallow frying pan. When hot, pour in enough batter to coat the base evenly. When the pancake browns underneath, turn it over using a palette knife and cook for another half a minute. Slide pancake onto a plate. Separate each with kitchen paper. Set aside, keeping warm.

3 Fry the bacon and onion for 5 minutes. Add mushrooms, cook for 5 minutes and season well. Preheat oven to 200°C/400°F/Gas mark 6.

4 To make the sauce, melt butter in a small saucepan, add flour and cook for a minute. Gradually beat in the milk. Bring to the boil; stir to a thick smooth sauce. Stir in mustard and half the cheese. Add half the sauce to the mushroom mixture with chopped parsley.

5 Place 1 pancake on a buttered ovenproof plate or baking sheet. Spread with some mushroom filling, put another pancake on top. Repeat, ending with a pancake. Sprinkle remaining cheese on top. Cover loosely with foil.

6 Bake for 10 minutes to heat through: remove foil to brown cheese, for 5 minutes. Reheat remaining sauce, adding a little milk or water to thin if you like. Cut pancake stack into wedges, pour over sauce and serve with heaps of freshly cooked vegetables.

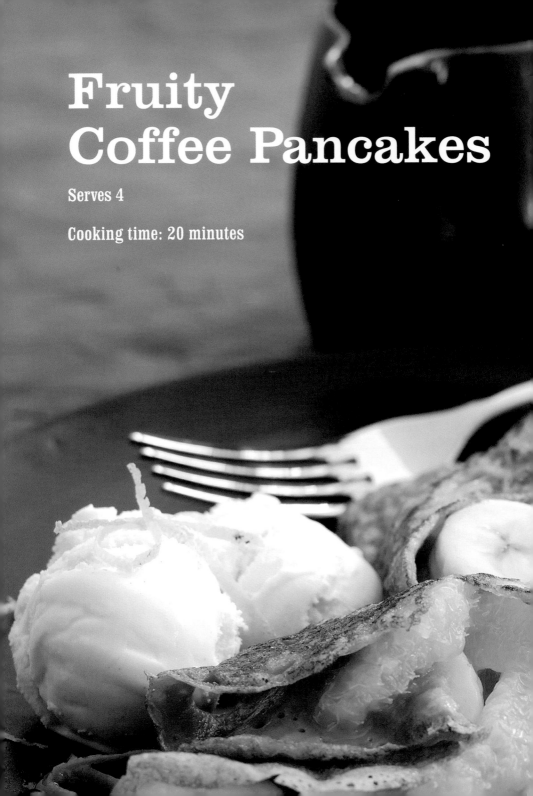

Fruity
Coffee Pancakes

Serves 4

Cooking time: 20 minutes

Ingredients:

- 110g (4 oz) plain flour
- 5ml (1 tsp) instant coffee granules
- 1 egg, beaten
- 300ml (½ pint) milk
- 25g (1 oz) butter
- 2 oranges
- 2 x 5ml (2 tsp) cornflour
- 2 x 15ml (2 tbsp) clear honey
- 2 bananas (peeled and chopped)
- Greek-style natural yoghurt to serve

Method:

1 Place the flour and coffee granules in a mixing bowl and gradually stir in the egg and then the milk to form a smooth batter.
2 Heat a little of the butter in a frying pan. When hot, pour in 3 tbsp of the batter, tilting the pan to cover the base. Cook the batter until the pancake moves freely, then flip it over and cook until the other side is golden. Repeat to make 8 pancakes, keeping them warm while making the filling.
3 Remove the rind from the oranges with a zester. Using a small, sharp knife, take away as much of the pith as possible. Holding each orange over a bowl, slice in between each segment to release the flesh and juice into the bowl. Mix the orange juice, cornflour and honey and heat in a small pan until thickened. Add the fruit.
4 Fold the pancakes into triangles and fill with the fruit. Serve immediately with the Greek yoghurt.

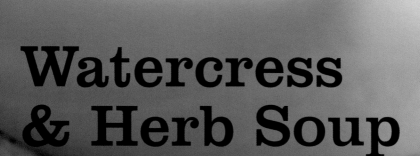

Watercress & Herb Soup

Serves 6

Cooking time: 25 minutes

Ingredients:

- 40g (1½ oz) butter
- 1 onion (peeled and chopped)
- 2 bunches watercress,
  (trimmed and chopped)
- 40g (1½ oz) plain flour
- 600ml (1 pint) milk
- 450ml (¾ pint) vegetable stock

- 15ml (1 tbsp) parsley
- 15ml (1 tbsp) dill
- 15ml (1 tbsp) chives
- 150ml (¼ pint) single cream
- salt and freshly ground
  black pepper

Method:

1 Melt the butter in a large pan and cook the onion for 3-4
  minutes. Add the watercress and cook for a further 2-3 minutes.
2 Stir the flour and cook for another minute. Remove from the
  heat and gradually stir in the milk and stock. Bring to the boil,
  stirring continuously, until thickened.
3 Add the herbs and simmer for another 15 minutes.
4 Cool slightly and then purée in a blender or food processor, in
  batches if necessary. Cool and chill. Stir in half the cream and
  season. Alternatively, return the purée to the saucepan and
  heat, but do not allow to boil, before stirring in half the cream.
  Serve chilled or warm, ladled into individual bowls with an
  added swirl of cream.

Macaroni Cheese

Serves 4

Cooking time: 25 minutes

Ingredients:

- 250g (9oz) macaroni
- 1 leek (trimmed and cut into chunks)
- 110g (4oz) broccoli (cut into equal-sized florets)
- 4 rashers streaky bacon (optional)
- 350ml (12 fl oz) semi-skimmed milk
- 3 x 15ml (3 tbsp) plain flour
- 5ml (1 tsp) English mustard (ready-made)
- 110g (4oz) extra-mature cheddar cheese (grated)
- salt and freshly ground black pepper
- 2 tomatoes (cut into wedges)
- 2 x 15ml (2 tbsp) parmesan cheese (freshly grated)

Method:

1 Bring a large saucepan of salted water to the boil and add the pasta. Bring the water back to the boil, cook for 5 minutes and then add the leek and broccoli and cook for another 5 minutes.
2 Meanwhile, preheat the grill to hot and cook the streaky bacon rashers, if using. Pour the milk into a saucepan and, over a medium heat, whisk in the flour. Bring to the boil and keep whisking to make a smooth sauce. Simmer for 4 minutes and then add the mustard and half the cheddar and season well.
3 Put a flameproof dish under the grill to heat up. Drain the pasta and vegetables well. Tip them back into the saucepan and gently stir in the cheese sauce. Spoon the mixture into the hot dish and sprinkle with the rest of the cheddar.
4 Arrange the tomato wedges on top and snip the bacon, if using, with scissors, into small pieces, and tuck them into the sauce. Sprinkle with parmesan and put the dish under the grill to brown the top. Serve hot with green vegetables or salad.

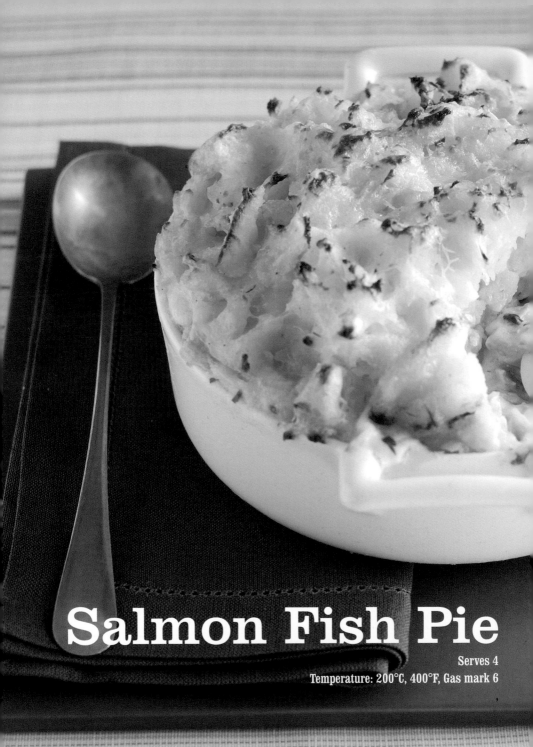

Salmon Fish Pie

Serves 4
Temperature: 200°C, 400°F, Gas mark 6

Ingredients:

- ¼ swede (peeled and cut into chunks)
- 3 potatoes (peeled and cut into chunks)
- 600ml (1 pint) milk
- 400g (14 oz) salmon fillet
- 350ml (12 fl oz) semi-skimmed milk
- 3 x 15ml (3 tbsp) plain flour
- 4 eggs (hard-boiled, peeled and quartered)
- 2 x 15ml (2 tbsp) cornflour
- 3 x 15ml (3 tbsp) water
- 2 x 15ml (2 tbsp) chopped parsley
- salt and freshly ground black pepper
- 50g (2 oz) butter (melted)
- 50g (2 oz) cheddar cheese (grated)

Method:

1 Place the swede in a saucepan, cover with water and bring to the boil and then leave to simmer for 5 minutes. Add the potatoes to the pan, cover again and simmer for a further 20 minutes or until the vegetables are tender.
2 Meanwhile, pour the milk into a saucepan and add the salmon. Bring to the boil, then reduce the heat and simmer the fish gently for 4-5 minutes or until the salmon is cooked. Remove the pan from the heat and use a slotted spoon to lift the fish out of the milk.
3 Remove any skin from the fish and flake the fish into large chunks into a 2 litre (3½ pint) ovenproof dish. Add the quartered eggs to the dish.
4 Mix the cornflour with 3 tbsp water. Bring the milk to the boil and slowly pour in the cornflour, stirring well to give a smooth sauce. Simmer the sauce for about 1 minute until it has thickened, then stir in the parsley and season it to taste. Pour the sauce over the fish in the dish.
5 Preheat the oven to 200°C/400°F/Gas mark 6. Drain the vegetables well and add the melted butter and seasoning. Mash the vegetables until smooth, then spoon them over the top of the fish mixture. Sprinkle the grated cheese over the top.
6 Bake the pie in the centre of the oven for 20-25 minutes until the topping is golden in colour and the filling is starting to bubble. Remove from the oven and serve with green salad.

Winter
Vegetable Soup

Serves 4
Cooking time: 40 minutes

Ingredients:

- 50g (2 oz) butter
- 1 onion (peeled and sliced)
- 225g (8 oz) parsnips (peeled and sliced)
- 350g (12 oz) leeks (trimmed and sliced)
- 225g (8 oz) potatoes (peeled and sliced)
- 750ml (1¼ pints) vegetable stock
- salt and freshly ground black pepper
- 300ml (½ pint) milk
- nutmeg for garnish
- flat-leaved parsley a handful, torn to garnish

Method:

1 Melt the butter in a large, lidded saucepan. Add the prepared vegetables and cook them gently for about 5 minutes.
2 Add the stock and season to taste. Bring to the boil, cover and then simmer for 30 minutes or until the vegetables are tender.
3 Transfer to a blender or food processor and purée until smooth, in batches if necessary.
4 Return the soup to the pan, add the milk and reheat gently. Serve sprinkled with freshly grated nutmeg and parsley and accompanied with warmed naan bread.

Index

Beef Bourguignonne	8	Quesadilla, Salmon	28
Beef, Stir Fried	16	**Quick & Easy Italian Frittata**	38
Cheese, Macaroni	56	**Rack of Lamb with Rosemary**	14
Caramelised Pan Seared Trout	22	**& Mustard Crust**	
Fillets with Lemongrass and		**Roasted Thai Style Red Pork with**	36
Chilli Honey glaze		**Sticky Coconut Rice and a Chilli**	
Crab Claws, Kircubbin Bay	26	**Dipping Sauce**	
Curry, Pork and Pineapple	42		
		Salmon Fish Pie	58
Fish Pie, Salmon	58	**Salmon Quesadilla with Cream**	28
Frittata, Quick and Easy Italian	38	**Cheese & Chives**	
Fruity Coffee Pancakes	52	**Sautéed Tender Pork Fillet with**	44
		Caramelised Apricots and a	
Honey Grilled Pork Sausages with	40	**sweet Garlic drizzle**	
Colcannon Mash and Onion Gravy		**Savoury Pancake stack**	50
		Soup, Watercress and Herb	54
Italian Steak Wrap	10	Soup, Winter Vegetable	60
		Spicy Prawn Salad	32
Kids' Kedgeree	24	Steaks, Topped	18
Kircubbin Bay Crab Claws with	26	Steak Wrap, Italian	10
Lemon, Garlic and Chilli		**Sticky Sesame Pork Kebabs with**	46
		Chargrilled Vegetables and Zesty Rice	
Lamb Chops with Honey	12	**Stir Fried Beef**	16
Lamb, Rack of	14	**Strangford Lobster with fresh**	30
Lobster, Strangford	30	**Linguini, Summer Vegetables,**	
		Roast Shellfish Oil & Chilli Gremolata	
Macaroni Cheese	56		
		Topped Steaks	18
Pancakes, Fruity Coffee	52	Trout Fillets, Caramelised Pan Seared	22
Pork and Pineapple Curry with Rice,	42		
Mango Chutney and Naan Bread		**Watercress and Herb Soup**	54
Pork Kebabs, Sticky Sesame	46	**Winter Vegetable Soup**	60
Pork Sausages, Honey Grilled	40		
Pork, Roasted Thai Style Red	36		
Prawn Salad, Spicy	32		